Dutiful Heart

Dutiful Heart

POEMS BY
Joy Gaines-Friedler

BRP
Broadkill River Press

COVER PHOTO "Meira" by Sarah Robinson Farkas
COVER DESIGN Barbara Shaw
AUTHOR'S PHOTOGRAPH Moti Friedler
TYPESETTING AND LAYOUT Barbara Shaw

Library of Congress Control Number: 2013948776
ISBN 978-1-940120-91-1

BRP
Broadkill River Press

James C.L. Brown, Publisher
Broadkill River Press
104 Federal Street,
Milton, Delaware 19968
E-mail: the_broadkill_press@earthlink.net

TABLE OF CONTENTS

ACKNOWLEDGEMENTS

Third Wednesday	"Arthropod," "For The Rain"
Driftwood	"A Canal in Southern Florida"
Michigan Poet	"Black Ice"
The Dunes Review	"Decent"
The Writers' Digest Poetry Award	"Jerusalem: At The Market In The Old City"
Controlled Burn	"Returns," "Snow Day," "Key School" "Domestic Violence," "One Must Have The Mind of Spring"
Natural Bridge	"I Come Stumbling In"
Bear River Review	"Cigar Smoke Rising" "Home Movie – Palmer Park 1962"
Silver Boomer Books	"Widow"
Montucky Review	"Without"
San Pedro River Review	"Detroit," "Harbors"
Arts & Understanding Magazine	"Test Trials"
The Patterson Literary Review	"Plaza Hotel Florida,1969"
MJHS Journal	"Neighborhood Watch"
Milk Sugar Literary Journal	"Bette's Choice"
2 Bridges Review	"Florida Wetlands"
Poetica Magazine	"Assisted Living, Caring For The Irreducible"
The Broadkill Review	"The Year of the Horse," "Tuesday," "The Holy," "Miscarriage," "Poem For Place"

Thanks to my cherished Michigan poetry community; to Mary Jo Firth Gillett, Russell Thorburn, Thomas Lynch, Keith Taylor, Ken Meisel, Terry Blackhawk, and my friend, Paul Winston, who loves poetry and doesn't write it. Special thanks to Barbara Saunier for her friendship, poems, and farmhouse bed. Thanks to *The Landscape Writers* in Holland Michigan whom I cross the state once a month to be inspired by, and to Colette DeNooyer for her generous spirit and that marvelous home on Lake Michigan. Thank you Kim Addonizio. Also, thanks to Celeste Rabaut for our *Meet & Work*s at Starbucks. Thank you Sid Gold for your skillful and spot-on editing, Barbara Shaw for your talent with design, and to Jamie Brown for trusting and publishing this manuscript.

Special thanks to Jack Ridl for his extraordinary humanity and inspiration, for teaching me the *art* of poetry, and for making me laugh.

Many thanks to my dear husband Moti.

Special thanks to Gerry LaFemina, who first inspired me by his amazing poems then became my friend and mentor. Thank you Gerry for spending pleasant hours talking poetry and life, but especially for playing ping-pong and letting me beat you once.

This book is dedicated to
NANCY WILLIAMS
in blessed memory

– Thanks Big Sista'

It is no little matter, this round and delicious globe, moving so exactly in its orbit forever and ever, without…the untruth of a single second.

–Walt Whitman

DOMESTIC VIOLENCE

When she said she was leaving him
    I couldn't guess why.
Just listened, watched her push scrambled eggs

around her plate, heard the clanging of kitchen staff
    and some other sound –
a hum of fear – am I making it up now?

When she said,
    It wasn't supposed to happen to me,
a tray crashed – I heard someone laugh

at my own failed marriage.
    I didn't understand
what she was saying – as though seeing only

the fur of wild things, the feathers of hawks.
    Danger wore a manicured mask.
It wasn't supposed to happen to me –

I heard a glass smash. I imagined a cuppah
    falling. I saw the white pillars of her porch
the perfect rows of roses

the neighbors shaking their heads;
    I heard book club gossip.
And now that she's gone?

What of those nameless insects
who make themselves so well known at night
    pulsing like blood

through silence, pulsing
like a tune I can't get out of my head, pulsing,
    get it? get it?

THE YEAR OF THE HORSE

The Chinese menu says I am born in the year of the horse
                    that I *need* people –
that I should marry   *early*.

Waiting for egg rolls, my friends change the subject
when I tell them how I never stood a chance –
that my mother's private lesson was,
            You kids are wonderful despite me.

I brace myself –
here comes what I know to be true:

They bring their mothers with them
    breaded and covered in a tender wrap.

As for marriage — I have done my hitch
but it kicked me
then took off running.

Like a horse, I am *a pillar of strength,*
a glutton for friendship.

I'm much taller than I appear:
            Go ahead – measure me
one hand at a time.

HOMELAND SECURITY

The auto plants are east of here –
broken, rusted,
abandoned like Chernobyl.

To the north, farms, where dinners include prayers
                             we never hear.

I'm immune from knowing
people who sign-up for the wars we keep hidden
like an economy.

Here, lawns get cut, leaves picked-up, the neighbor's kid
has made it into law school.

I'm making lists; planting Rugosa Roses.

Yet, there is a coyote roaming the neighborhood.
        Someone asked, have you noticed
the missing rabbits?

Yesterday, a waitress from down-river complained
about her son, said, *the army will help him grow up.*

I lined the salt up with the pepper.

I don't live in a no-other-option area.

DETROIT

I once photographed Coleman Young,
twenty years the mayor – he made swearing an art form,
talked in similes, said,

Racism is like high blood pressure,
the person who has it doesn't know he has it
until he drops over with a goddamned stroke.

It was the day my husband moved out
        and took his power tools with him.

That night a friend offered distraction,
two tickets to Kool and The Gang.

What have the suburbs to offer me now?
The city feels comfortable in my hand
like a found rock.

Coleman said, *Courage is one step ahead of fear.*

I think of the sound of factories in the voice
of an old boyfriend from The Cass Corridor –
cocoon of his attic bedroom, mattress on the floor,

candle light and books in that long season of snow
shining in the window – Coleman's city –

Canada faultless in the glass towers along the river.

Come on – celebrate good times…

The word *Renaissance* is painted across this city's
solid surface. The flourish hides its wounds.

SPRING

In memory of Linda

A bullet blast through a cardinal.
Wings. You. Shattered.

You left
    when the days were swollen with cottonwood
    and a primal mind.

It's hard for me to admit
            this inconsolable grief. It's Spring again.

Our plans still sit on my calendar.

I find plumage
everywhere.

I shiver at the gunning of basswood from
            a downy,

I find in the bright sky
            the smell of gunpowder.

This never ending raucous of
bird life,

powerful and fragile as a nest,
                        breaks me.

It's Spring.

I will go outside, remove the cracked canvas
from the lawn furniture,

put out the smiling hippo that measures rainfall.

I will notice the lilacs in bloom and the small pools
of water, and I will wait.

BETTE'S CHOICE

Praise the way Bette
chooses to die here;
the way she sits
unyielding
in her yellow chair,
socks hanging choked
in the dresser drawer,
bed sheets soaked
with sweat and urine,
bits of food
on the nightstand;
praise how she ignores
the incessant ring
of the telephone,
the doorbell's buzz,
how she is done
with doctors, treatments,
percentages; praise
the batteries
that hold on in the remote
so she can sit
in her faithful privacy,
watch *Bewitched*, smoke
through the pain;
praise the conviction
that clings to her
like light to the moon,
like nicotine to her walls;
praise her beautiful
belief when asked,
Bette, what's going on here?
and she answers,
Nothing.

CIGAR SMOKE LIFTING

Another night of wind pours through the lost
   ash trees. Mom stumbles through
Bingo, says she is *doing the best she*

can. On her bookshelf your army
Discharge Pin, your prized possession, lays
enshrined in the bottom of your cigar box like a flag
folded under the letters from war-weary
girls who thought you might love them.

How you never imagined this, Dad. Surprised
     you said, that forgiveness would come to you
in your last days. I have returned as though a
jury to proclaim you *not guilty.*
    No need to pray for exoneration
    it's enough that you have stowed your

knife of words. The box still smells of smoke and
late nights on the back porch with your brother,
     whiskey busy in your glasses,
     talk of business,
mom lost in her Solitaire.

Now, I have returned to burn my diaries.
    I can't remember which I first fled –
our closed bedroom doors, or the click
    of those cards.

    Here is your 1941 report card.
    I am not surprised by the check-
pluses of your *citizenship* grades – aren't we all
quick to prove how well we can work in the world,
    hide the private from the public? Ah, but no longer
    a refugee I have arrived

reverent, as you sit
silent in your chair like an unspoken grief. Your
temper, tempered.

Unsteady, is how I cling to you; a wayward
vase, the way a bird curves its tiny bones around
                                        the twigs of wobbly
branches. These days I hold to
        the time we have left, and to the
X's on your schedule of medications.

Yesterday, I saw a tiny girl dance on her father's feet,
        remembered my own delight of lace
        foam around my ankles;
    my patent leather shoes. How light
    I must have felt as I held to you

  like the flickering flame of your
Zippo, those summer nights. Cigar smoke lifting.

TUESDAY

Mom has stopped answering her phone,
insists the walls are ringing,
says it's Sunday when it is Tuesday,
says the parking lot is a river that has spilled
                                        its borders.
She whispers
They're mad at me because I called the police.

I whisper back. I whisper back

and tell her that I am not like the good Rebecca
at the well of unbidden offering. I am more like a flag –
full of faithfulness. Full of wound.

I've too rewritten days – taken out the endless shuffle and
slap of card hitting card, of waiting out silence with silence.
I make days into threads that tether me to forgiveness
and offer no certainty. I can't let truth
be only truth.

No one is mad at you, I tell her.
No one has ever really been mad at you.

THE HOLY

Another holy morning – the sky chalk dust.
I'm drinking Columbian, the cat purrs his companionship,
the voices of two walkers reach me, distant
                    and wholly decipherable. I am grateful
for the hummingbird still showing up this late
in September.

I push my cat's paws off the keyboard,
                    he puts them back, I push,
he thinks it's a game and notches up his pleasure.
Outside I spread thistle and bread, see how close
the deer have tracked, hope they find food this winter.

The suet cage has gone missing.

Later, I will pay my mother's bills, spread them
on the table, label a new file: FAMILY TRUST.
I get dizzy when I turn my head. I get dizzy
watching the birds swoop and stash seed. I get dizzy
when I see my missing father's face
                    in the cumulus of my mother's cloud.
She's been falling.

A phone call last night from someone who found her
in the hallway, another from her, telling me how she
waited to be rescued.

                    Alone, she keeps repeating.
The apples fall hard. In another week
the hummingbird will surrender
the window and what is left of the nectar.

This morning she is still here – her wings pumping
like a dutiful heart.

ARTHROPOD

A spider survives in the corner of the bathroom
                        between the toilet   and tub.
I've startled it into reclusion only to find
once again   it seeking   what it seeks.

I want to keep this spider
                                alive
for it reminds me of some   persistence.

Last night when someone asked
what do you do? I wanted to ask   when?

Some days I do nothing   but pay
                        my mother's bills – stand guard
against the tangle of dementia that threatens her.

Other days   I pay my own.

Sometimes I go outside and slip a shovel
                                into the soil – dig through
loam and compost, plant iris –
try to keep things alive.

Mom calls, claims
someone   has stolen her   blankets.

I want to recede.

I wonder how long a spider's life is?

I could turn the vacuum on that spider
I could sweep it from its web – stomp it
but there is something   impressive   about its survival.

Today a new discovery:
     Mom has given away   her credit cards.

I don't know what a spider actually does
     or what it   remembers.
It's enough   that it's here.   That it's lasted this long.

ASSISTED LIVING
CARING FOR THE IRREDUCIBLE

I

Two women in wheelchairs argue:

Don't touch me
What? Why?
Get away from me – you're an idiot,
I could kill you.

A timeless battle: One who wants only love.
One whose hard grief is a multitude of grief,
a stone box of grief.

II

Maybe we have practiced caring for them
the way we handle the heavy scrolls of Torah,
kiss them with our frail lips,
with our weighty book of prayers.

We discover our names in them, drape them
with breastplate, plait them in velvet.
They are scrolls scribed by their lives.
They hold all the shalts and shaltnots inside them.
They are lifted heavily from their wheelchairs
then set down in their beds like something holy.

We memorize the Kaddish
then close the heavy curtains.

III

I love thoughts and ideas, love music, love
these women silent or silenced by age who sit in wheelchairs
against the walls like soldiers with no enemies, stultified as
though past worries were vain indulgences. They sit without
husbands, those that held them at night,
their lives lined-up along their dressers in frames –
each a small prayer – dear G-d, a son. Amen. Dear G-d a
Bat mitzvah, a granddaughter, a trip to Italy. Amen.

IV

The lady at the front desk wears Florida all over her.
She is hot pink and yellow and whispers to me,
Your mother is so happy to see you,
as though this secret is a key to unlock the past,
as though unlocking it would rewrite it.

Florida reminds me that I have curly hair,
that the ocean is its own planet,
that humans can recreate what should belong
only to cockroaches and very large spiders,
that I am often right and frequently wrong;
I love as simply as I despair
and feel too easily the suffering of others
as though I know the secret to life is to make it through –
joy is one way. Velvet whispers of Torah is another.

V

If one of the irreducible asks you what floor she lives on
remember the way she once knew consolation and to
console, or drank rum and laughed heavily. *Tears are*
wreathed in dense beautiful layers. May we all find acceptance
in change. Amen.

VI

They are rows of trees lining the boulevard
They are silver and gold lining
They are frail crystal cups
They are collectors of small treasures
They are the flat surface of blue water
They are the western sky

VII

Sunlight breaks through the heart here.
It can barely raise its head,
its neck weak as an after-harvest stalk.

The small nurse with hands of a prophet claims,
If I can make one of them happy
just for a moment – it's enough. Your mom…
smiles every morning. See? See it? That's what I get.

VIII

There are two sides to this life:
The side you nurture, and the side you fail.
The child you inspire, and the one you reduce.
Sacrifice. And the women you turn hard against.

IX

Sometimes they get violent. Your mom though, she always smiles.

X

Mom has a missing tooth. Her smile both warms
and concerns me. It was an implant, a single denture –
a thing she could never keep track of. Like her wedding
band, it's gone missing. Life is like this – grief for
the small lost things – joy in the not caring. The past just
wants to be the future. The future cares little of the past.

XI

I am a seer and I walk into walls.
I put my right foot in front of my left
push the button for the third floor
push aside the smell of urine and waste.
I hate my mother's missing buttons
the stains on her pants. I'm sorry
I showed her a recent photo of herself
her long gaze of recognition –
What do you think? I asked her.
I should see a dentist. She said.
Does the Torah suggest the proper
way to respect someone else's prayer?

XII

These discoveries are not new to me.
in the small sheets of hospital beds I discovered
love is the devotee of suffering.
And when the doctor with eyebrows of palm trees,
and his disciples in white coats, entered the children's ward
like Moses – prayers rose up all over the place.
I became the mother child of all the children.
I became the mother child of my mother.
I have always been my mother's next day.

XIII

I know you wait for me
the way the bench in the park waits for shade.
Your vow is silent and unmovable.
Our love recreates itself the way sand moves,
but the beach remains, the way every wave
is a new wave of unceasing waves. Amen.

There is a crack in everything. That's how the light gets in.

– Leonard Cohen

BLACK ICE

The night has become a car slipping silently
Into a ditch after touching another
Then recoiling from such intimacy.

What falls does not fall
But rather thickens,
        but we knew this
When we left the house –

The day started out so

Vulnerable.

The night has become a police car
Herding drivers off the freeway.

Like a cataract
Sleet claims the windshield.

Make it home – everyone's cold mantra.
One more mile.
One more time.

Make it home –
Along a known
Yet, unexpected hazard.

We are saying nothing.
We are cleated.
We are knuckling through.

SABBATH MORNING NEW YORK CITY

There are people who live entirely without community
he told me as I walked with him to Shul. He didn't notice

my lack of uniform, my unpaid dues. Didn't notice
my well-groomed flight feathers, my refugee status,

my preference for quiet places.
He didn't notice I pay only rent.

Maybe I never let myself be a part of anything
that would remind me that I've never been
                                    a part of anything.

I keep hidden my empty calendar, my missing
family portraits.

I told him that sometimes we seek blindly
that which we need.

His community forms around ritual.
I didn't walk through the door he held open for me.

Instead, I got on a bus with strangers –
watched the landscape grow increasingly familiar.

"WINS ABOVE REPLACEMENT"

You think you have a memory; but it has you!
        –John Irving (*A Prayer for Owen Meany*)

Baseball was ruined for me
when my brother hit a line drive
across the yard into my head.

My right temple a throb of isolation.

His laughter a training in choice.

This was my first lesson in grief –
and how we stumble toward affection
strewn with weeds and trees unhewned.

I staggered into the living
room – Mom the shape of a question
curled on the couch.

Eventually guilt may call you *out;*

may even cause you to offer something
you deem precious – something
tangible – money perhaps,
or a stuffed armadillo for example.

What I remember is
what's always been withheld.

But this isn't about redemption
or even empathy. This is about boys
sacrificed by their fathers' lessons
of fists,

and what my mother taught me
when she opened her eyes and said,
Leave the boys alone.

LUNA MOTH

Rarely seen. Lives only five-eight days.

A cabin porch, one light, everything still
as West Virginia granite —

the trees close-in around us like spires,
and memory. A train's distant coda
hums, sanctify, sanctify, sanctify,

when an moth, wings the size of a man's hand,
urgent and delicate as a first kiss, shows up
like an answer.

How can anything as short-lived as this
be so luminous?

I want you to think what I think,

see it as amazing   all that work to get here
attach it to something we both want.

I want us to be full of mouth and wings.

Say something. Say, *bodacious,* say, *cocoon,* say,
chance, say, *want* and *have.* Say, *us.*

Say, *there must be a god.*

WIDOW

for Joanne

I've learned to put salt in the softener, to pay
the bills with no reluctance. I've learned
to fill the empty sections on the calendar.
I can phone a roofer should I need to,
take the car in for alignment. Every day I wake
to the same light through our bedroom window
to the same absence, to the same alarm.

FLORIDA WETLANDS

From the boardwalk egrets and woods ducks
feed their young

the sloughs swell
and spadderdock bloom yellow
such lovely   work.

What I try to detach myself from

I've let in even further.

Not the swell of nature that remains
a kind of *them* and *us*
but the way their distress suns itself
  in the small clearings
  alligator skinned and toothy—

the way I can't keep my mother
from drowning in her bog of dementia.

Doing her laundry today was
strangely satisfying – load, dry, fold
load, dry, fold

and I think of work – and how we must.

I think of the bars across from the factories
back home in Detroit –
once filled at quitting time
how Mom talked fondly of *those days,* everyone
sweating it out for a pension.

            Wood ducks swim in and out
between those floating flowers.
Tonight they will settle in under sawgrass and moonlight
            the way I will sleep on the couch – hoping

tomorrow will be the same.

DESCENT

Today Dad started morphine, a few drops
under the tongue. He at his computer,
the Nasdaq under the flashing cursor,
yes, like a heartbeat, yes, like a warning,
checking his stocks, the weight of tumor
pressed against his belly.

I am not there for this. Home,
in the backyard, filling the feeders,
listening for cardinals, feeding the ferns,
digging, trying to keep things from dying.

Above me contrails scar the sky;
an illusion of clouds. They will mix
with rain, form droplets that will burn
cattail and pine needle.

Descent. What was once so far away,
a tiny tumor of glistening airplane,
is now the sound of grinding metal;
an approaching engine.

A chickadee flutters airborne
scattering black oilers to the ground.

REVIEW OF THE ORDINARY

A breakfast of Swiss cheese and toast Sunday morning.

God and politics on television.

AIDS and Domestic Violence are not just part of my vocabulary
        they are the next door neighbor who broke in
        through the basement window.

He didn't take what he knew was already broken.

I once left a bag of weed on the kitchen counter.
While we were out walking someone broke in
and left two watermelons.

Twenty years after the divorce I realize, I've given up what I need
as many times as I've needed what I don't have.

Here is the body. Remember it.
Here is the dent in the fender from the drunk night.

Here is the door. A bit of WD-40 could fix that.

MISCARRIAGE

Last night the barn across the street
burst into flames.

First sound that rumbled like a moan.
Then terror.

The fire screamed the way a scream
remains silent through other screams.

There was no stopping this.
Time traveled back toward birth –

a revelation of its dubious skeleton.
Suddenly lifeless – an empty space.

The morning drifted in ash.

RETURNS

It's coming upon a year my friend sat
    Lotus style
in her Hospice bed, said, *It's so terrible*
and, *Finally, I understand love.*

And, my neighbor called to say his wife
    is leaving him.

I admit slugging through with only
a feathery slip of a word —
Sorry.

That exoskeleton that can grow around me
    keeping sweetness out?

I'm sorry for that too.

When my friend, thin as a wing,
stared at me, then said,
This must be so hard on you,

I shook-off that protective layer.
I let that be her last gift to me.

My neighbor keeps everything clean,
                fixes everything,
has dropped his wife's name, turned her into a pronoun.

She's living with someone else,
he says without my asking.

Every morning a chickadee flings itself
against the window – fighting its reflection –
defending against itself.

Today, at the mail box, my neighbor said,
She's not coming back.

THE POLISH CAFÉ

for Jack Myers

Reading the menu, I am dipping in and out
of an unforgiving feeling. I am smoke
by the window that disappears then reappears between
light and shadow. Self-conscious, dark haired,
I feel I'll be discovered, *handed a yellow star, tattooed.*

Maybe, I'll order pierogi
so much like my mother's kreplach,
dumplings stuffed with meat, and I think
of how the selling of kosher food became a crime,
how the butchers went missing,
how the locals spit in the ghetto wells.

And right here in this family restaurant
filled with smokers and drinkers I want to stand up
and yell. I want to tell the couple at the table next to me
that *She was only thirteen for God's sake —*
snatched away, thrown into a cattle car,
war put inside her

that still, night whistles wake her
weeping for her mother – transferred
like those dirty dishes, to extermination camps.

I can get crazy like this, let my imagination fill
and stuff, think I owe the dead something. Come on,
these hungry drinkers and smokers have nothing
to do with history except to live in the safety beyond it.

They're here to eat Kielbasa.

The waitress holds a pen to pad, a menu under her arm.
Was it her mother who turned-in my starving uncle —
watched him shot for trying to steal a potato
from her compost pile? And just when I'm thinking,
Christ,

the day's become a ripped shirt, a terrible hunger,
forgive, forgive, orders are orders, just order,
I notice above the bar a portrait of John Paul II,
his cotton face, his hand raised in a gesture of what? Humil-
ity? Finite Distance? He blesses this place

like one who sees life in terms of *them* and *us,*
as one who comes out on top in the knowledge of that.
I consult my menu, smell nutmeg infused onion
and the repulsive stench of burning flesh.

I order potato pierogi without gravy, tell myself,
just finish your dinner and get out.

POEM FOR PLACE

Here is a poem for all the cities
I've never lived in; for the misty country
I cannot claim; for all the painted fences,
school yards, named mountains, creeks
and silos that are not mine. Here is to places
that hold someone else's wheaty memories.

Here is to cathedral spires – their scolding
safety – to bustling corners, familiar
strangers, and the awful beauty of blight.
Here is a love poem to noise and walk-ups,
smoky viaducts, horsey, viney, Southern Baptist,
cactus, big family, military- based, home-schooled,
living with grandma places. This is a love poem

to the lighting and humidity braided into you,
whose voices, noises, hurricanes, and drought,
whose soil, air, and smell are the triple helix of you,
wrapped like unopened iris around sediment
and rock, chance and circumstance. Here
is a poem for all the places I cannot know;
the shock absorbers where bodies ripen; the places
that leave us brittle and nourished as bone.

JERUSALEM:
AT THE MARKET IN THE OLD CITY

A small woman
In the clothes of Krakow

Before the darkness
Before the heart tattooed
With its grief

Shmatas
My mother calls them
Ragged, patched together,
Reclaimed.

She is wearing her exile,
Her lost mother's
Memory, waving her flag of
Small comfort.

Whatever happened
Keeps happening;

Keeps her from escaping
The night howl of train whistles

Though now she is smiling;
Her smile keeps clean
The golden stone of Jerusalem.

She is holding a tiny wallet,
A single bill in her hand,
Buying macaroons,
Something sweet for the table.

When I think back on it now, it's the juxtapositions that are so moving to me.

– Susannah Sheffer

HOME MOVIE -
FLYING A KITE IN PALMER PARK - 1962

We are in our winter coats, light snow falling, still Fall,
trees not fully abandoned by leaves, Detroit not fully
abandoned by the leaving. My father is tethering
string to kite.

My nine-year-old sister is jumping up and down,
her knit cap tied with two stringy balls under her chin, the
wings of her coat flapping. She is suspended and plaid.
She can't wait for the kite to leave my father's hand.

My mother's hands are in her pockets. She is wearing pants
and pearls. She doesn't notice the kite. She is shuffling foot
to foot. She remains unfocused, blurred. My mother wants
to return home, tell secrets in Yiddish.

My brother is seven, he wants to hold the string, wants my
father to let him hold the string, wants my father to make
the kite go higher, my sister to stop dancing, wants my fa-
ther to let him hold the string, wants me to stay away

from the kite. From everyone. My sister's arms are kite tails.
She is twirling in circles, bobbing up and down, she is
caught in braided turbulence. I am five. I am standing
quiet, hands in my pockets.

I admire the balconies off the porches, the pitched roofs,
the old trees, the swing sets in the back yards. I admire
the picnic tables and their scratched messages. I already
know that there are ghosts of families there; there are

families not like ours. I know, there are families not like
ours. My mother is shuffling foot to foot, her mouth is
saying *come-on, hurry up, it's snowing.* We are in the city. We
are in Palmer Park. The kite is trying to leave.

ONE MUST HAVE A MIND OF SPRING

Mom has forgotten to fear – forgotten
to insist on unopened blinds.

She's become petal soft,
a white peony in full burdened bloom.

She no longer worries about blankets
of late burning frost, denuding winds,

is unconcerned with what day it is, has no unease
from the hawks waiting, watching

the building of nests. She once invented the unmanageable,
assumed every key would be lost, dreamed of rocks,

damp wings, claimed *it's all so hard,* claimed thieves
had stolen her underwear, her blankets.

Mom's mind is untangling.
Someone said she's become *delightful.*

The Poplar have released their seeds
filling the air with cotton.

THE PLAZA HOTEL, FLORIDA, 1969

Fledglings, we sang harmony
by the elevator where the acoustics
made us sound gothic, flutish, sound like road trips,
microphones and Stratocasters.
We were peasant shirts, tie-dyed, sandaled,
about to smoke cigarettes, reek of dime bags,
and fringed suede jackets. We were patchouli oil,
Dead Heads, moody, blue, and sex. We
were choices about to be made. Afraid
from all the wanting, we sang
of freedom we craved, feared, already had.
Sixteen, what did we know of loss? What
did we know of roads miles away
and someone to miss us? We sang
like the Haights and Ashburys,
like something was about to burst open
in us, spread like pollen among flowers
applauding in parks, our long hair
parted in the middle, earth style,
earth shoes, earth reaching up in us.
Nothing yet polluted. We sang
like wind sweetened with cannabis
and chance – a train whistle's harmony,
deep and throaty, we sang
the way park-dogs worked on Frisbees,
leaping, grabbing, offering, offering,
we sat on the floor near the elevator,
Joanne and me, pulling the sea-soaked air
into our lungs, pretending, preaching,
singing about surviving something
we hadn't yet hazarded, neither homeless
nor forsaken, just five hundred miles from home.
Five hundred miles. Five hundred miles.

VIET NAM WAR MEMORIAL

Left behind on Koh Tang Island
three young Marines: fate unknown.

We face an impenetrable wall.
At close range the names
                    dominate everything.

The sound of choppers blading the air
cut cleaves in the vinyl disks of a generation –

Highest state casualties: California.

I had a copper bracelet – the name of a soldier
embedded – MIA – Missing In Action.

I wore it two years

until the day it went missing.

Highest per capita casualties: six boys
Beallsville Ohio — pop: 475

There is nothing to wrap our arms around here
We can only –
            face ourselves.

The mind is malleable.
We begged them to stop this war
                a blade held at the throat.

There is no returning shadows
                    to the rose.

The night the helicopters rose over Hanoi
I saw the faces of the saved —

                                  an unholy ascension

and wondered who was being left behind.

KEY SCHOOL

Amy Lewis died from a brain tumor
so we plant a tree for her
outside our 4th grade classroom
our coats on – it's almost winter.

In another week, Larry Blank's voice
will hush our classroom by yelling
the president is dead.

We'll learn where Dallas is and watch on new
color televisions that slow train, those
beautiful faces of grief.

This is how I learn love.

Last week another friend sat Buddha-Style in her
Hospice bed, aware of each breath as consciously
as a kiss. Staring at me she said,
I know this is hard on you.

I vaguely remember Amy. On a field trip
to the zoo I sat beside her on the bus. We passed
Amy Joy Donuts and giggled at the odds of that.

We could never know

that one day, and it would be soon, I would
stand on the wrong side of the window, planting a tree
I imagine will grow, create shade, release

seed. I think of Amy the only way I can: Amy Joy,
the name as sweet as two little girls
bouncing on green seats.

NEIGHBORHOOD WATCH

The street we walked home from school was bare
                              and orderly,
trees still the twiggy saplings of suburbia,
the neighborhood a slender girl with an expense account,
a new purse to match each outfit.

The gardens lacked the lush gospels of nature –
only a few daffodils grew outside Mrs. Goddeson's house.

What did I know of flower bulbs, or the hands
                              that planted them?

I left the sidewalk, crossed her narrow history of lawn
and pulled at the thick stems that would not release.

Someone was sure to see me.

Someone was already marking me.

Feet sinking into soil, I pulled at the stubborn flowers,
                    until I felt something tear.

Frightened and willing I held in my hands the whole of it;

yellow flowers torn from their roots,

some terrible death, some beautiful life.

MISSING

for the people of the Haiti earthquake 1/12/2010

There is no address
to send this package,
no porch to savor spiced rum,
no blankets to get through the night.
There is only this shaking fear.

Did someone say a prayer
for you? Or You?

I wasn't scared
says a ten-year-old –
she sits among the others
pulled like tubers from the wreckage

waiting for the missing.

There were houses made of
wattle and daub.

Now, a woman,
her two children,
live under a tent
made of bedsheets.

She has a broom.

She has a broom,
and she is sweeping the floor.

TEST TRIALS

9/18/89: Heard on TV tonight: Q is very promising & kills HIV in test tubes, but warns Not For Human Trial. Well I'll try it!

From the journal of James Kerr

What if the word *deficiency* had no need
to coexist with *auto* and *immune*. Or, you
had been born five years later, and the cocktail
caught up to you. Maybe

we would be mocking The Emmys, choosing blue
swatches for wall paint, laughing about that time a bee
flew into your car – we nearly lost our minds. Finally
one of us, was it you? opened the door. We looked at each
other and laughed a full five minutes.

There are 745,000 results for AIDS CURE in a Google
search – and not one of them is.

Now I'm looking at the blinking cursor, feel
the words *curse* and *cure* in those perfectly straight
heartbeats – right here you would give yourself away
and insist: *Never straight. Only forward.*

They say there are parallel universes
                where the thinking of a Thing makes it so.

What if I think you smoking a Tareyton, a cup of coffee, no-
tice that slight tremor in your hand. Now I'm thinking: you
never met that guy, didn't make that date, had a flat tire,
called me up, asked, *What about Bridgewater Blue?*

UNIVERSAL PARADOX

Never argue with bruises.

Or the complicated ease of Roger Federer's forehand.

A kiss is never just a kiss.

Here is my friend alone again –
his wife blaming him
for what is untamed in her.

He said, *I love you,* meaning,
I have a plan for showing you.

She heard, *I need you,* meaning,
she's no good at folding sheets.

Here is her goodbye on the table
next to the loveseat.

At the hospital, after another fall,
Mom believes she's been arrested.

She bends the known and unknown
into the shape of a heart.

Today four friends went out to lunch
because they heard someone else was diagnosed.

A hummingbird will chase away a chicadee.
But a bee will chase a hummingbird.

AT THE MARKET IN AKKO, ISRAEL – A WEDDING

Ancient stone sea port – witness to Bronze
and Iron eras, to Napoleon. Akko's boulders
lay their history in deep-throated sea music.

Sometimes, it's hard to be American
full of independence
      giddy with liberty.

You Americans have no idea
what it's like to constantly feel threatened.

I laugh. A Constitution
is an idea only; *The Melting Pot*
separates as easily as this sea sifts silt.

Here, there is a motion of history. Women sweat
under the cover of the Hijab as they shop for spiced tea.
What is freedom?

I want to go to the man selling mangos,
ask if he hurled rocks during the
last *uprising,* or worse,

planned the strapping of explosives
to the bodies of young women –
then I think of the hard news from home,

Dr. Tiller, killed in his church in Kansas.
From what do we gain our pride?

I turn to my nephews, already Israeli soldiers,
ask if the army teaches them to hate. They both say no
and I'm more confused than ever.

I hear the movement of wings from a dove,
look in the dark spaces for it,

when suddenly, rhythmic clapping, song
rings through the narrow stone walks
and around the rough walls.

Men in jeans, Nikes, voices perfect and unfamiliar
accompany a groom in red and gold on horseback.
Such happiness is universal. The women follow –
I have already forgotten their head cover.
As they pass me, me with my silly camera, one gestures
Join us. Come. Join us. She pulls me in.

WITHOUT

I'm lying in the back seat
  without a man
    to kiss
Just listening
to robins, some sparrows,
  a cardinal chipping an evening sermon.
The garden of lake
  breathes in the fading day – blue
    as a sealed iris.
I am here
  contemplating
    the way sunlight bleeds
through maple leaves,
and the way I left you
  because you cannot hear
  the homily of trees
      or know the sweetness of tapped sugar.

FOR THE RAIN

I want the day to start slowly –
gray even, let things
                    emerge,

let the pine trees become pine trees.

I want the rain to seep insatiable
                        into desire, pull
its clouds over the day, swell

sedum and yearning and remind me
of some   connection

like that pair of swallows
enjoying that   small depression
of water.

I want just enough light   to see
the river's tributaries
        around your eyes –
                        a serious mood
in them.

Let the river flow river.
Let the rain murmur rain.

Yesterday, the light
                    was like a tragedy

so I sat in it awhile.

I COME STUMBLING IN

If this isn't love then why return
to the photo of two tulips intertwined that way.
Why this thought:
> *Grace comes as an obstacle to belief.*

Why these dreams of deadbolts and falling doors.
Why you on my speed dial. If this isn't love

why the urge to cook long brewing stews and decorate
with birch bark. Why the impulse to get drunk.
What is it that is trying to flee from my bones.

Why is every fortune cookie a coincidence,
every sun-rooted day a thief, every lucky couple
a word for *sorrow*, a word for mouth, a dress
falling to the floor.

If this isn't love why MapQuest the batting cages,
                              why play Solitaire,

why not just pull down the barn and be done with it.

If this isn't love then why show up
                              like light through the pines,
why give five dollars to the guy on the off-ramp,
why endure the flag in its half mast, or grieve
the squirrel who rolled itself out of the way.
Why write, *To the darkness. You'll see.*

I am not so good at this. I admit. I flee
from the cat's crouch like goldfinches at the feeder.
I leave the dishes dirty. Still, I return to you, broken,
ready to break again.

BECOME A TREE
for Chico Hernandez

Go deep into woods. Stand in the sling
of dappled light. Listen to the woody
wisdom of robins work out their chords.
Feel the green breeze blouse over your
skin, the moist heat of community, a
society of saplings and the old stag-heads
reaching for the same sun. Imagine
leafing out. Now, imagine holding an almost
weightless nest in the crook of your arm.

SORRY FOR YOUR LOSS

There is a mother-idea in each particular kind of tree...(Byron)

The thunderstorm last night
caused more than one bird to rebuild.

I'll look for lost nests later.

You seem to have been very close to your mother –
mine has always been hidden
behind a tangled braid of branches.

That's the thing – some loss is tangible
some is more a kind of borer beneath the bark.

I learn this about trees:

*Restoration typically requires more
than one pruning to develop strong tree structure.*

I remember asking – how is your mom?
you said – *ninety three.*

If I find one, I'll add another nest to my collection,

be impressed by what is possible.

HARBORS

The rivers are in their place.
The barnacles and fish are in their place.
The winds that cross the ships that bring baseballs,
    bearings, resin barns, are in their place.
There is a new pope.
There is a melting icecap.
There is a tea shop by the boardwalk.
The lost balloons are in their place.
There are people in their place.
The distant islands look close while close
    eyes look distant.
There are children who find lost heroes between
    the slats of wood. They are in their place.
A man wants money for drink, a woman gives it
    to him. They are in their place.
The cormorants and grebes are in their place.
The people shopping along the wharf, sipping wine,
    forgetting...are in their place.
The lighthouse reminding us of threat is in its place.
The rocks and pylons that hold our world
    above the dark enormity are in their place.
There is a far off depth and a shallow presence.
There is grass that grows despite salt and asphalt.
The landings are in their place.
The dredgings are in their place.
The bells and clangs and ropes are in their place.
The ships that carry our burdens, our demands
    are in their place.
And always something arrives. And always something leaves.
And just beneath the water something grows. All
    are in their place.
And for all the commerce, for all the captains,
    there is a current both dangerous and calm.

Joy Gaines-Friedler studied photography at The Artography Academy in Los Angeles then returned to Detroit where she photographed local dignitaries and children. After the deaths of her two best friends, one from AIDS, the other from a Domestic Violence murder/suicide, she returned to school to study literature. She has been awarded both academic and literary prizes, including The Litchfield Review Poetry Prize and The Tom Howard Poetry Prize. Her work has been an Honorable Mention and Finalist in The Paterson Poetry Prize, The Paumanok Poetry Award and The Allen Ginsberg Poetry Prize. She also received scholarships from, among others, The Cranbrook Writers Guild and The University of Michigan's Bear River Writers' Conference. She teaches Advanced Poetry and Creative Writing for non-profits in the Detroit area. Through Common Ground she has the honor of facilitating writing workshops with young adults "at risk" and families of victims of homicide.

This is Joy's second full-length poetry collection. Her first book, *Like Vapor,* was published by Mayapple Press, 2008.

CPSIA information can be obtained
at www.ICGtesting.com
Printed in the USA
FFOW02n0832120117
31102FF